Where the Cartpath Ends

Where the Cartpath Ends

the poems & drawings of

Barnacle Goldstein

WHERE THE CARTPATH ENDS

ISBN 979-8-9887019-1-0
Ebook ISBN 979-887019-2-7
Printed in the United States of America.

www.barnaclegoldstein.com

Where the Cartpath Ends

TO GOLF (A TOAST)

Here's to the game that keeps us coming back for more,
And here's to the shots after which we don't yell "Fore!"
Here's to the quest to beat our all-time best score,
And here's to the heights to which we will one day soar.

You are a game that gives, but one that also takes,
You are a game that punishes us severely for our mistakes.
You are sinister at times with your trees and your lakes,
And you show us no mercy outside your white stakes.

But there is greatness that we all strive to achieve,
To pull one last trick out from underneath our sleeve.
And you are a game that allows us to still believe,
Even though we know we are just being naïve.

So "To Golf" I say as I raise my glass,
May all of our shots in life find the short grass.
And when things gets rough and troubles amass,
We will have you to thank for our dignity and class.

WHERE THE CARTPATH ENDS

There is a place where the cartpath ends
and before the scorekeeping begins,
and there the greens roll true and pure,
and there the sunburns have a cure,
and there the shots fly like on tour
to six feet from the pin.

Let us leave this place where we mark an eight
and the bogies keep piling on.
Past the traps full of treacherous sand
we shall putt with a putt that is steady of hand,
and watch the ball roll exactly as planned
to the place where the cartpath ends.

Yes we'll putt with a putt that is steady of hand,
and we'll watch the ball roll exactly as planned,
for the great shots, we mark, the great shots, they land
at the place where the cartpath ends.

BREAKFAST BALL

You step to the tee and take a deep breath,
Off to the right is certain death.
To your left there is nothing but trouble,
It will take a miracle to score less than a double.

But you can relax and take an aggressive swing,
For you need not worry about a thing.
You have a crutch on which you can fall,
Because in your pocket is a breakfast ball!

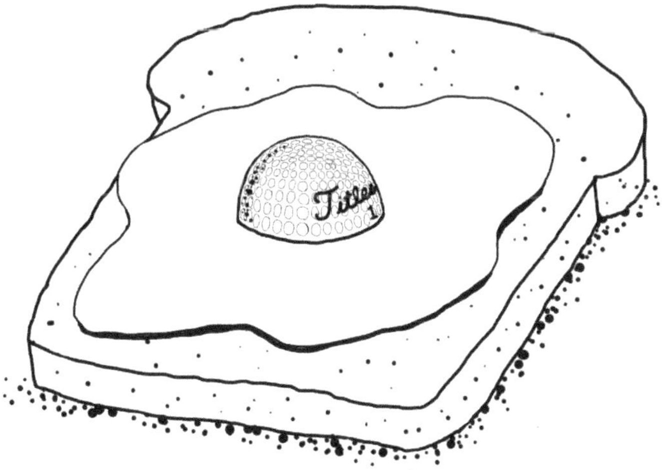

TRUE STORY

OB, OB and then twenty-three.
Yeah, one time that happened to me.

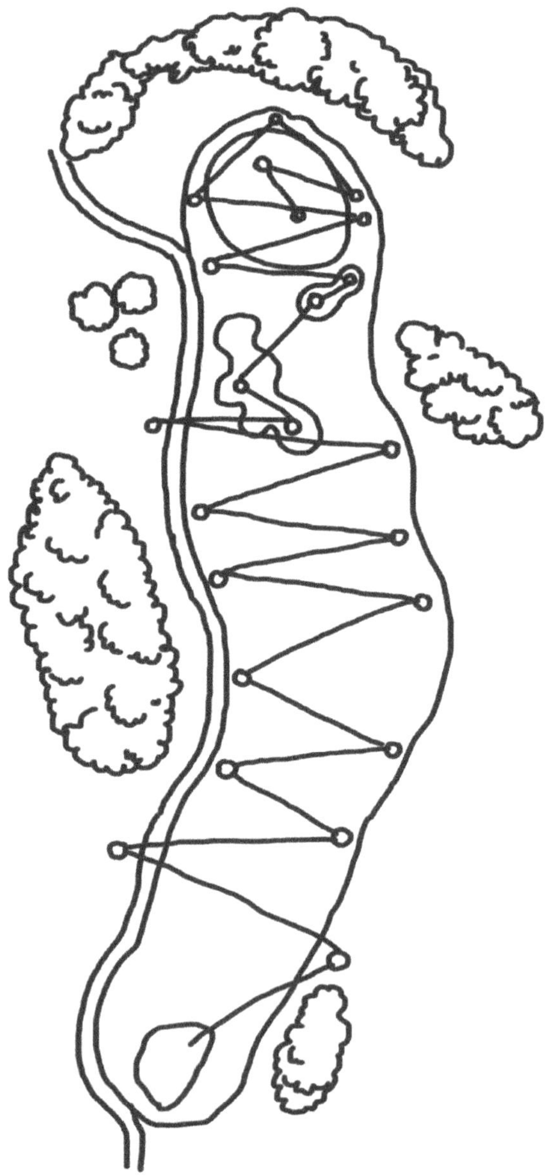

TOP 10 GOLF SECRETS

There are 10 secrets every golfer should know,
Since this is a list let's get on with the show!

- Your driver can be your worst enemy,
  Don't be afraid to hit a hybrid from the tee!

- Practicing six foot putts can be a bore,
  But it's by far the best way to improve your score.

- Control your temper and don't be in a hurry,
  No one makes shots when they're full of fury.

- Miracle shots are not what the game is about,
  Learn to take your medicine and just punch out.

- Believe in each and every one of your shots,
  Nothing good can come of negative swing thoughts.

- Drinking and driving doesn't just apply to your car,
  Stay dry on the course and play the 19th at the bar.

- You can't be illiterate if you want to succeed,
  Spend time with your putts and learn how to read.

- Don't worry about distance, just hit the ball straight,
  You manage to do that and the results will be great.

- Get to know your golf ball and communicate with it,
  Teach it to listen when you yell "bite" and "sit!"

- Above everything else just remember this one,
  Golf is a game so just go out and have fun!

TRUST ISSUES

I remember on the hole before
You told me that you got a four.
But there on your card I see
You seem to have marked a three.
Now that I know how you score
I don't want to bet you anymore!

CART PARTNER

You pulled your drive and I did too,
Off we go to Timbuktu.
You sliced it right and so did I,
Let's give the other side a try.
As a cart partner I'm pretty great...
Unless you happen to hit it straight!

GOLF 101

Golf can make you feel elation
But mostly you feel frustration.
Because for every great shot
There are a hundred that are not!

THE WIND BENEATH MY SWING

My head is down just as I was taught,
"Keep your left arm straight" is my only thought.
My feet are lined up, my address is correct,
But I still have no idea what to expect.

A terrible slice or a god awful hook?
When it comes to bad shots I wrote the book.
And there's one result that we can't dismiss,
There's a very good chance I will swing and miss.

Yes, "The Whiff" isn't just a baseball phrase,
I've had my fair share in my golfing days.
For some players this result is the rarest,
But with me and my game I'm not even embarrassed.

I've come to embrace it like a celebrity,
My playing partners always enjoy the hilarity.
Golf is just a game and I'm pretty darn sure,
There's no future for me on the Senior Tour.

So I laugh and get ready to try it once more,
I've only added one shot to my score.
Maybe this time I'll hear the sound of the ping,
Instead of only the wind beneath my swing!

THE ZONE

You don't know how you got there
But you never want to leave.
It's a feeling like no other
One you never thought you'd achieve.

But alas you find you've made it
To the finest place you've known.
Enjoy your time - it won't last long;
Welcome to The Zone.

When you're in The Zone the world is yours
And anything can be.
Nothing is impossible
When you step up to the tee.
Fairways look like football fields
And greens welcome shots with glee.
And the cup size looks gigantic
Like a perfect double D.

And then seemingly out of nowhere
You find you've left The Zone.
The fairways start to narrow
Balls land in grass that's overgrown.
You can't find the sweet spot
Your shots are fat or thin.
And the hole looks like a quarter
You can't get the ball to go in!

We hope you enjoyed your time there
We don't know when you'll be back.
The Zone doesn't take reservations
So until then you're still a hack!

THE NEW DRIVER

My new driver isn't working out,
My new driver fills my head with doubt.
My new driver was a huge mistake,
My new driver's in the bottom of a lake.

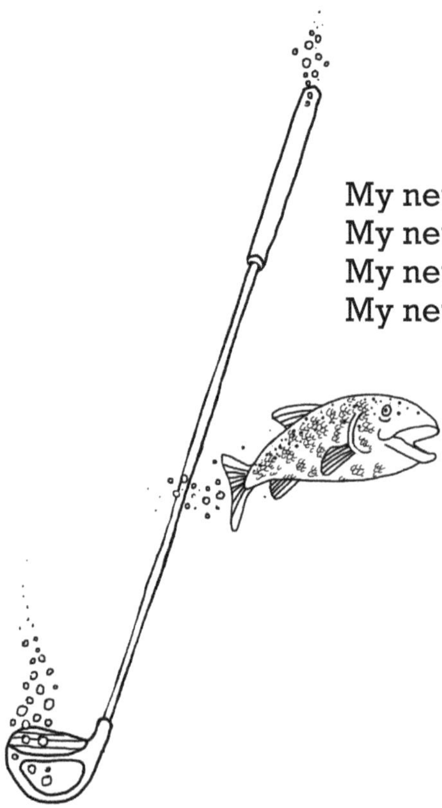

THE WEEKEND

It's Saturday so get out and play
You don't have to work today.
And so there's nothing that forbids
Unless you have a wife and kids!

THE ILLITERATE CADDIE

My caddie needs a tutor to teach him to read,
And brush up on physics to teach him about speed.
When he says it's left to right I know it's not true,
He thinks downhill's level and doesn't have a clue.

He says that we are putting on Poa annua greens,
But I am certain he doesn't know what that means.
He then advised me that I am putting into the grain,
But I don't believe that means anything in his brain.

He says the wind is blowing, so go on the attack,
The only problem? The wind is at my back!
When he finally give me his line I am mystified,
Then I drain the putt!
How?
I took the opposite side!

WHEW!

Off in the distance a man yells "Fore!"
You duck for cover and hit the floor.
A ball whizzes right over your head,
If you hadn't ducked you would be dead.

THE HUNGRY COURSE

This golf course feeds on golf balls and its appetite is strong,
If you only brought a dozen balls they won't last very long.
You'll need to carry more balls than a necklace full of pearls,
There's hungry trees, hungry rough – even hungry squirrels.

Two-thirds of the world is water and this course is in that vein,
Forget the cart, you'll need a boat to navigate this terrain.
Water is everywhere you look, you see more blue than green,
Forget the boat, to find your balls you'll need a submarine!

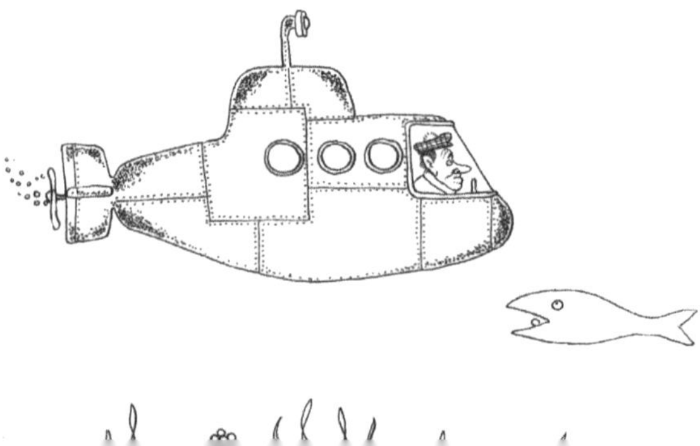

But on the balls that don't splash you shouldn't feel too secure,
You may think you're in a fairway, but you can never be sure.
There are rolling hills that roll off cliffs, rough six inches thick,
And trees that hold onto balls you never thought would stick.

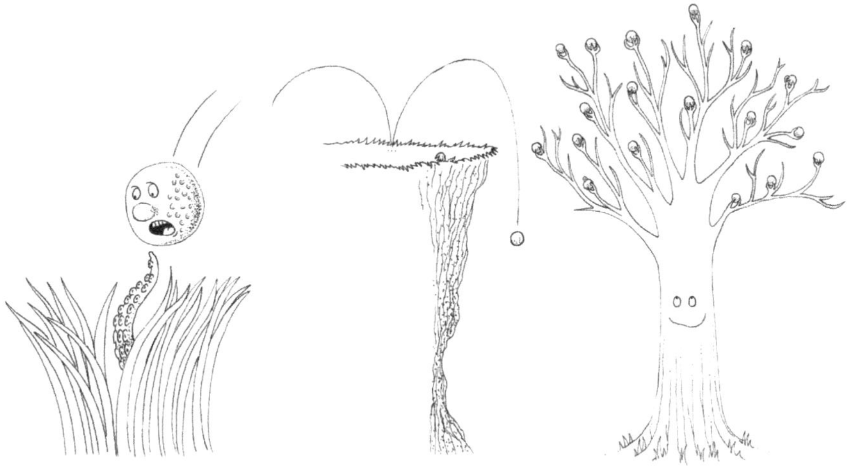

Yes this is a hungry course and it feeds on Pro V1s,
Callaways and TaylorMades – plus Top Flites just for fun.
So if you want to try it make sure you bring a full supply,
Because this course is the place where golf balls come to die.

TEE TIME

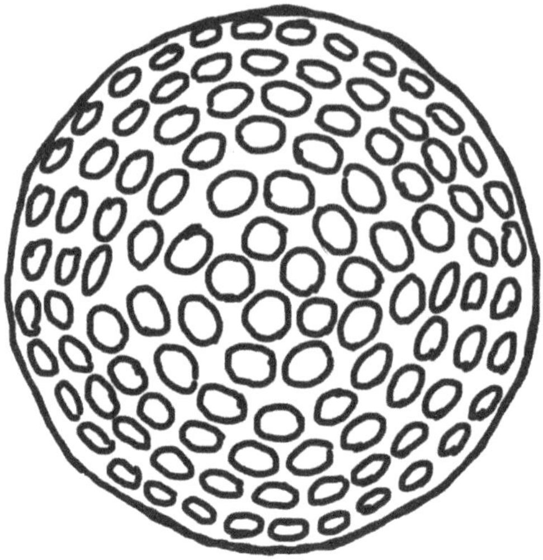

IAMAGOLF

TEE

H
I
T
T
H
E
B
A
L
L
N
O
T
M
E
!

DANGER

BEWA
R E
THE
S N
O W
MAN

He'll ruin your score!

THE CAST & CREW

Hello, I'm The Valet and I'll be parking your ride,
We'll take care of you clubs so just head on inside.
Don't worry about a thing, they'll be safe and sound,
Go on into the Pro Shop and enjoy your round.

Hey, I'm Gary and I'm The Pro Shop Guy,
Have you given the new TaylorMade driver a try?
Maybe you'd like to buy a shirt or hat from me?
No, just the green fees? Then head on out to the tee.

Hi there, I'm The Starter and I'm the one in control,
I'm the one that stands between you and the first hole.
My job is to stop those that would try to cheat,
You ain't getting past me unless you show a receipt.

Hi guys, I'm The Cart Girl, are you enjoying the links?
You fellas look like you could use a few stiff drinks.
I've got water and soda, beers and all the rest,
But Kettle One bloodies are what I do best.

Gentlemen, I'm The Marshall and I am here to say,
Have fun out here, but keep up the pace of play.
And don't let that ol' Cart Girl serve you a double,
She's been known to get guys like you into trouble.

RING-RING, it's Your Boss and there's a situation,
I don't mean to bother you like this on your vacation.
It's just that there's some issues that are starting to grow,
So if you could maybe come into the office… hello?

Hey there fellas, it's me, The Cart Girl once again,
It looks like I've come across some very thirsty men.
I think I've got a good idea for you and your buddies,
How about I make another double round of bloodies?

Um, hey there guys, it's us, The Group Behind You,
Would it be too much to ask if you let us just play through?
It's just that some of us have places we need to go,
And for the last few holes you've played really slow.

Whoa there Big Jim, you don't need to start a fight,
We're not in a hurry and that guy was quite polite.
Besides, we're out here golfing and this is hardly a race,
We'll let 'em on through and get back to our pace.

Friends, it's The Marshall and I was called to this hole,
You'd better get your buddy there under control.
'Cause I've got rules that I am obliged to enforce,
If you don't straighten him out, you're all off of the course.

Gents, it's Big Jim and I've really gotta say,
I sure am sorry that I let my temper get away.
Let's finish up this round and I'll finish my cigar,
And then I'll buy each one of you a drink at the bar.

Hey Chief, I'm The Bartender, how did they roll?
No worries, there's no bogies here at the 19th Hole.
You fellas look like you've already knocked back a few,
How about I start with a round of water for each of you?

Hello Sir, I'm the GM and you really need to leave,
And while you're at it please wipe that drool from your sleeve.
We have already called and made arrangements for a cab,
But don't you dare leave this place without paying your tab.

Hey Bro, I'm the Taxi Driver, you don't look so hot,
I'll bet you wish that you had passed on that last shot.
I promise I will get you home safely and discrete,
As long as you promise not to vomit in my back seat.

Hi Honey, it's Your Wife – so let me get this straight;
You think that you can just stroll in here four hours late?
I'm gonna let this slide, but you see, here's the rub,
I just called and canceled your membership to the club!

TECH BOOM

'Twas a time when a 3 wood was made of wood.
'Twas a time when you had to hit a 3 iron good.
Now, that's ancient history,
Thanks to technology!

SO CLOSE

The round of your life wasn't to be
Your final score was one-o-three.
You don't want to complain or whine
But just once you'd like a 99!

STILL AWAY

Another shot, I've taken a lot,
That wasn't my goal, damn this hole.
And now I hear you say,
"You're still away."

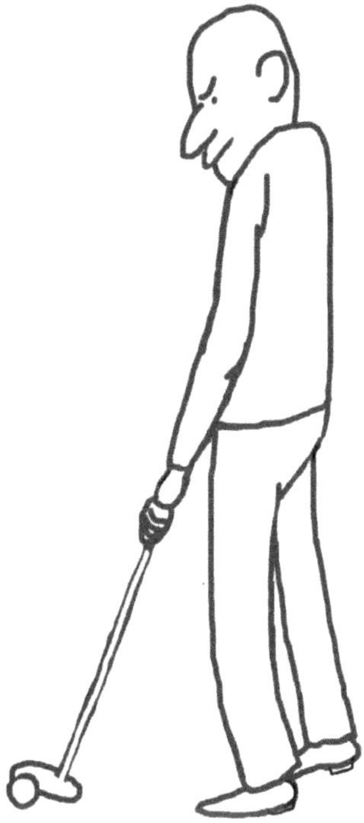

SHORT GAME

You practice your distance,
With endless persistence.
But lately you're skipping,
Your putting and chipping.
Sure, the ball goes far,
But you don't make a par.

STAIRWAY TO SEVEN

There's a score in my head that glitters like lead,
And I'm riding a stairway to seven.
My first shot goes awry, sailing sideways through the sky,
And it's not what you'd call a slice of heaven.

Below a tree by the brook, I feverishly look,
And the rough is laughing with thickness.
There's a feeling I get, when I think my ball's wet,
And my spirit is crying with sickness.

But alas I find the ball, deep in the rough which stands tall,
And my only chance is to punch out of it.
So I stand and do my best, aim my shot to the west,
And I yell at the rolling ball to "sit!"

It rolls through the fairway, in the opposite rough I lay,
And I'm determined to claw and scrap.
This rough it bites hard, it steals many a yard,
And I chunked it right into the sand trap.

So there I lie in three, up and down to save bogie,
But I catch too much sand and start to cringe.
I barely clear the edge, rolling gently off the ledge,
And somehow trickle onto the fringe.

This putt will take some skill, it's thirty feet and downhill,
And I'm fearing the chances of a three putt.
So I trust what I read, careful to control my speed,
And I feel the face of my putter close shut.

I pulled it really bad, then I got really mad,
As I watched it roll far past the hole.
Now I'm deep into trouble, just to save a double,
I'll need to pull off a fifteen foot roll.

The putt rolled out straight, 'least I won't get an eight,
But I needed it to run just a little more.
Two short feet away, finally something goes my way,
And I hear the sound that I have longed for.

With the ball in the cup, this hole is all wrapped up,
And I swear that I'll forget this disaster.
I write a seven on the card and I listen very hard,
As the golf course, it echoes with laughter...

And I'm riding a stairway, to seven.

SUPERSTITIOUS SAM

There are many things that Sam believes
And none of them make any sense,
He has lucky socks and lucky sleeves
And always carries frankincense.
Before each shot he taps his toes
And does a waggle with his hips,
He tugs his ears and rubs his nose
And then he licks his lips.
He has stacks of tees he won't discard
More lucky pennies than a fountain,
He keeps a stack of old scorecards
And they're taller than a mountain.
Sam has grandiose ambitions
But as a partner he is no fun,
Because after all his superstitions
His score was 101!

SHOCKING CONCLUSION

You don't know pain,
Until you've golfed in the rain,
And felt your hamstrings tightening,
Then got struck by lightning!

SECURITY RISK

$2500 in the trunk of your car
Could all be gone with just one crowbar.
So watch your clubs like a hawk
Cause they don't make a golf club lock!

PUNCHED GREENS

You arrive at the course and don't know what's occurred,
Cause when you booked the tee time, no one said a word.
From the first tee everything appears as planned,
'Till you get to the green and find an ocean of sand.

See, the greens were punched and the fight wasn't fair,
They look like they got mauled by a grizzly bear.
And then after the bear they were impaled by a bison,
With a finishing knockout punch delivered by Tyson.

To call these greens unplayable would not be a reach,
It's like putting on the actual shores of Pebble Beach.
No matter what you can't control the break or the speed,
Which makes these awful sandy putts impossible to read.

You finish your round and let 'em know it's brutal out there,
To which the pro shop guy shrugs and says "Buyer beware."
So the next time you book a round, don't dare take a chance,
Be sure to get the status of the greens in advance!

RANGE CART DRIVER

I've got a thousand balls to collect
But that part will be easy.
I know exactly what to expect
And I'm starting to feel queasy.
Because when I drive my cart out there
The situation will turn dire.
I'll breathe in deep and say a prayer
Because I'll be under heavy fire.

Yes it's true, I'm in a cage
That is designed to protect me.
But there's 30 golfers on a rampage
That are all out there to dissect me.
I see them sneer, I see them smile
With violence in their eyes.
I don't know why they're so hostile
Or why it's me they brutalize.

If you have ever been abused
Then you can sympathize with me.
I'm so dejected and confused
And suffering from serious PTSD.
But wait! If I ignore protocols
I can create a key omission;
I could just not pick up the balls
And they'll run out of ammunition!

THWARTED

The sky is clear, for golf that's great
But the temperature is twenty-eight.
Still you'd bundle up and go
If the course wasn't covered in snow.

OLD MAN WINTER

Old Man Winter you are welcome to get going,
I've had about enough of you and your snowing.
So kindly move on and get out of my way,
Because I have lots of golf I need to play.

O CADDIE! MY CADDIE!

O Caddie! my Caddie! our fearful round ain't done,
We're coming down the stretch and we trail the lead by one.
The air is dry, the greens are fast, the gallery is excited,
On this par five we hit a drive that had them all delighted;
But O no! no! no!
O what a huge mistake,
A layup was fine, where was my nine?
A three wood in the lake!

O Caddie! my Caddie! Rise up and take the blame;
Rise up – for this is all your fault – it will be your claim to fame,
The gallery is hissing, but why should they boo at me?
For it was you, not I that said, "Go for it" so confidently.
Here Caddie! dear daddy!
You said we'd bend, not break!
Is this just some dream on this course,
A three wood in the lake?

My Caddie does not answer, his face is cold and pale,
A picture for a poster with a caption reading "Fail."
Why did my caddie do this? Why did it end this way?
My caddie looks right at me but there is nothing he can say;
This is no dream my caddie!
We are both fully awake,
And we will never live this down,
A three wood in the lake.

NOT DONE YET

You're old and you're tired
You could go any day.
Soon you'll be expired
But you've got courses yet to play.
So go on out and have a gas
Enjoy your round at Pebble and Sawgrass!

MY MISTRESS

Honey, I love you, but I have a confession I must make,
I wish it didn't happen but I made a big mistake.
I thought it was a fling at first, I thought it wouldn't last,
I thought I would get over it but the feeling hasn't passed.

I know I have been distant and getting home too late,
This double-life is killing me, it's too tough to navigate.
Yes, there is another - and yes, I've fallen hard,
I never saw it coming and it caught me off my guard.

Before you grab that baseball bat I have to say one thing,
My mistress isn't human, I can't buy her a ring…
You see I fell in love with golf, but I still love you too,
There is lots of room in my heart for each one of you.

What's that you say? That's enough? This is the last straw?
Well don't forget your second love, here's a gift card to the spa

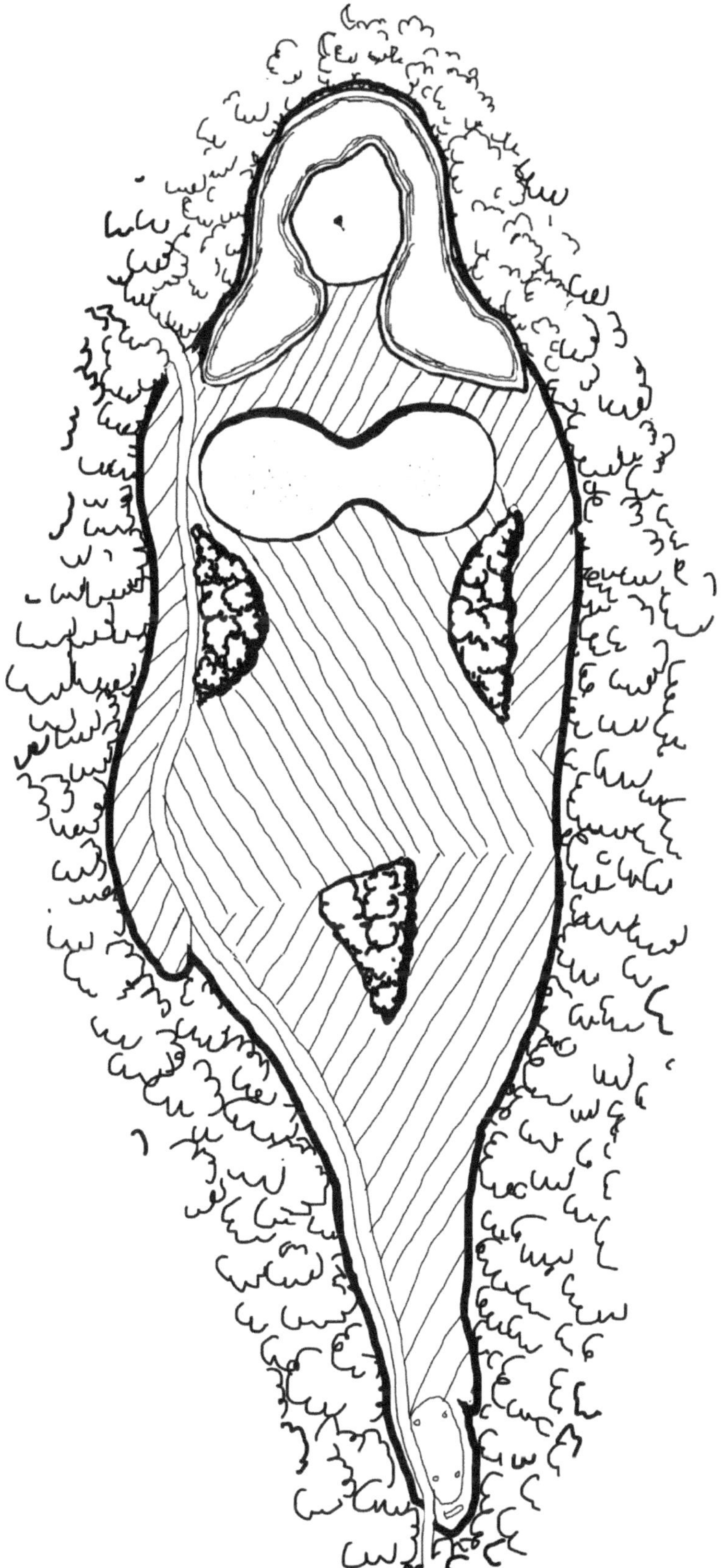

WHEN TO PACK IT IN

You set your goals
On 36 holes.
But after a day in the rough
18 was enough!

MULLIGAN'S ISLAND

Hey little buddy
Let me tell you a tale,
About a three hour round
That turned into a snail.
Things were fine at first
Everything was great,
Until we hit the turn
And saw what would await.
I'd heard of island holes
Like Sawgrass seventeen,
But never one like this
This was quite obscene.
The green is barely visible
A postage stamp is bigger,
I know this course is hard
But this is excessive vigor!
The pin looks far away
My gun says it's one-eighty,
My odds are better to spin a globe
And land my finger on Haiti.
But I tee it up anyway
And I kiss my ball goodbye,
Because I know with certainty
There's no way it's staying dry.
As it sails through the air
I think it might find dry land,
Because on any other hole
I'd have a putter in my hand.
But this is Mulligan's Island
And I know I'm in deep trouble,
I try three more times in vain
Then quit and mark a double.

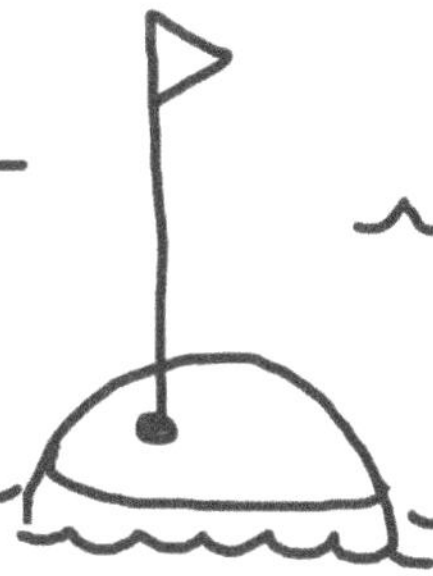

SWING THOUGHTS

They creep inside your head
And there's nothing you can do.
They fill your soul with dread
Because they're stronger than you.

Swing thoughts can be good
But mostly they are bad.
You'd control them if you could
But your mind's not ironclad.

"There's trouble left" "right is jail"
Aren't the best, but they're okay.
Remembering a bill you forgot to mail?
Is a bad thought on your takeaway.

There's angry wives and angry bosses
These are bad swing thoughts.
They can lead to serious financial losses
And tie your stomach into knots.

So take a breath and clear your mind
And find your place of zen.
Because if you do you just may find
You can hit it straight again!

MAMMA ALWAYS SAID

Life is like a box of ProV1s...
Expensive!

MAKING A MESS

One swing, two swings, three and four
Hello green, I'm at your door.
One chip, two putts, then two more
Mark a ten for my score!

KRYPTONITE

My drives are ferocious,
But my putting's atrocious.
Drive for show, putt for dough?
My bank account is getting low.
I'm the greatest golfer you'll ever meet,
Until I have to putt from three feet!

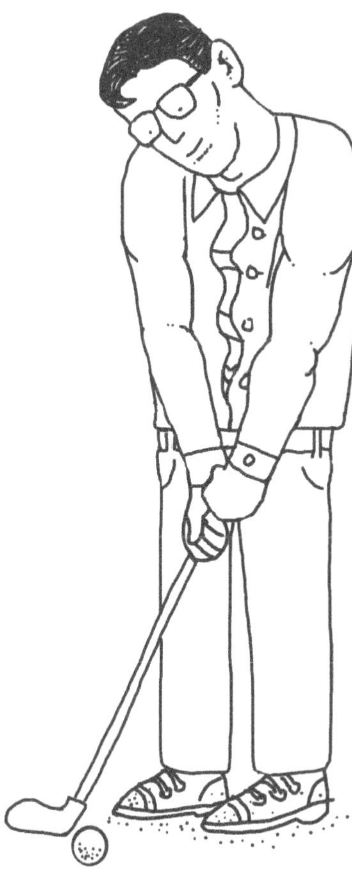

KA-BOOM!

It was a perfect day on the course,
I hit each shot without remorse.
I shot a birdie and lit a stogie,
I hadn't had a single bogie.
And then it happened, I lost control,
Ah, the dreaded blow up hole.

INDEX MANAGEMENT

I know this putt's for par,
But I already won the hole;
I'm playing in a match,
So stroke play's not the goal.
I'll make it look like I'm trying,
So that no one will know,
I'll shoot a pretty good score,
But I won't go too low.

"Oh darn, I pushed it,"
Is what I'll say to play it cool,
Even though I missed on purpose,
You know I'm not a fool!
I've got a member guest next month,
This could be our year,
But there's too many sandbaggers,
So my mission is clear.

I'll play some rounds with my old clubs,
I'll putt out with my wedge,
I'll do what I gotta do,
because I need a hedge.
I don't want to be this guy,
but it seems the only way,
Everyone else is doing it,
so honesty doesn't pay.

Am I a ten? Am I a nine? It depends on the day.
Just beware because a net sixty-one is always in play!

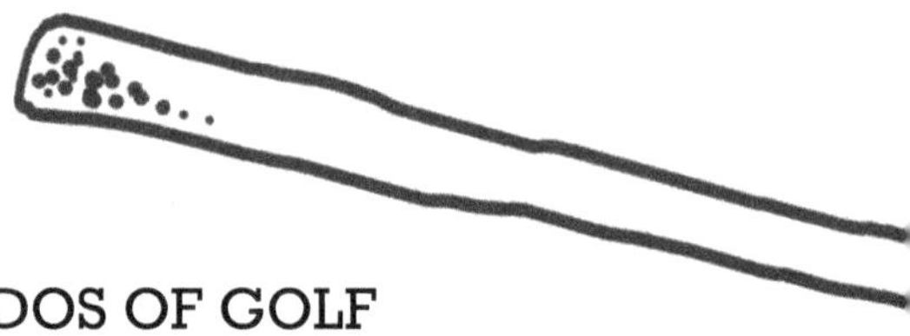

INNUENDOS OF GOLF

When something isn't big enough
It often comes with shame,
Which is why the PGA
Has been pushing to "grow the game."
And golf could use a boost
Since Tiger lost his skills,
The game needs the equivalent
Of a bottle of blue pills.

But Viagra and Cialis
Run commercials on every station,
Alongside all those ads
To prevent frequent urination.
But what the game really needs
Is a youthful infusion,
And so to create that
We need to clear up some confusion.

You see, if I was new to golf
I would have ran or laughed,
When another man approached me
To learn the stiffness of my shaft.
And I'm as progressive as the next guy,
But that only goes so far,
When you bet you can sneak it in the backdoor
For a drink at the bar.

Or if you invite me out to play,
But I learn there's just one rub,
That if I want to come again
I've got to join your private club.
You hype the beauty of the clubhouse
And the history within the walls,
And the convenience of the caddy
Who is there to clean my balls.

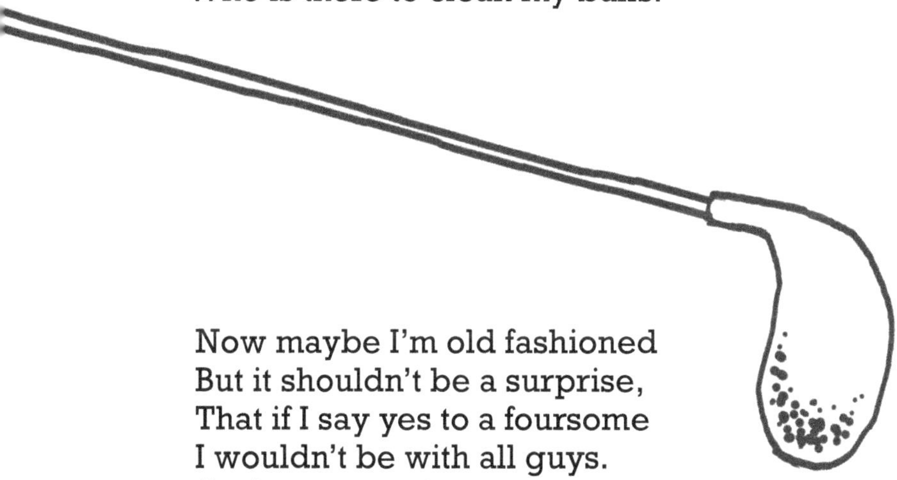

Now maybe I'm old fashioned
But it shouldn't be a surprise,
That if I say yes to a foursome
I wouldn't be with all guys.
And no matter how many there were
I wouldn't feel in control,
If one of the guys kept yelling
"Just put it in the hole!"

So I appreciate your compliments
And I hope it's not a joke,
I'm just not sure what to do
When you say you love my stroke.
But golf seems like a game I'd like
And I know I could have fun,
I just think until I learn the lingo,
I'll stick to rounds of one!

HEY MAN!

Hi, I'm your 3 iron, how do you do?
I didn't take that shot, it was you!
Aw man, really? Again with the throw?
And down the fairway I go…

THE LOST BALL

I've been alone for so long
I've lost track of the days,
Like a sad country song
Or a rat in a maze.
It feels like yesterday
Back when I was free,
I was announced "in play"
And I was placed on a tee.
I flew through the air
Like a bird in the sky,
I didn't have a care
Until a shot went awry.
I landed in a shrub
But I couldn't shout,
I saw the tip of a club
But it didn't scoop me out.
Then time started flying
And it sure went by fast,
Then they gave up trying
Because three minutes had passed!

So now I'm alone and dirty and scared
Wishing I had been from an owner that cared.
So remember my story because there will come a day
When you abandon my brothers...
Just to keep pace of play!

WHAT THE?

You line it up, it looks alright,
Just outside the cup, two inches right.
A perfect stroke, a perfect roll,
Is this a joke? It missed the hole!

GIMMIE GIMMIE!

"That's good, right?" shouldn't need to be said
Because a two-foot putt can get in your head.
And if there's one thing you don't want to weather
It's grinding out a putt that's inside the leather.

But your opponent says you need to putt it out
So you have to put aside all your doubt;
Step up and focus with all your might
%*#! - you pushed it right!

GOLF CLUBS 4 SALE

I have golf clubs for sale and I think the price is right,
I paid a fortune for them, but now I want 'em out of sight.
How much do I want for them? How much do you got?
If you can take them right away it won't cost you a lot.

No, this isn't fraudulent and no it's not a trick,
It's like a bad relationship, those clubs and I don't click.
Maybe they will work for you and things will turn out great,
But those clubs and I have grown into a special kind of hate.

See, the driver always slices and I don't mean just a little,
Not even once has it found a fairway in the middle.
The three wood and the five wood are equally as bad,
They are both responsible for the worst shots I've ever had.

The three iron, forget it – oh, you want to know why?
The only time I hit it I almost killed some guy.
The four iron is a mess and don't talk about the five,
Let's just say that club is very lucky to be alive.

The six iron always slices and the seven always bends,
The eight and nine spray all over, the trouble never ends.
And then there are the wedges for the gap and for the sand,
Never once have they hit a shot the way that I had planned.

And the putter, oh the putter – you can take that first,
But it's only fair to warn you that I'm pretty sure it's cursed.
If you can make a three putt with it consider yourself great,
In my last round I had a hole in which I putted eight.

So that's the story and the tale of why I'm selling cheap,
If you think you can do better I respect your faithful leap.
You'll never find a better price either online or at the store,
Now get those clubs outta here!
I don't want to see 'em anymore!

GETTYSBURG DISTRESS

'Four score and seven shots ago,
My father brought onto this course a new low.
He played bad here last year and this was the sequel,
Proof that all golf swings are not created equal.

Golf is a battle, but not in the literal sense,
Until my father graces the course with his presence.
The shot was misfired and went ninety-degrees,
And brought an unsuspecting golfer to his knees.

It jumped low and fast and bounced right of his head,
It was not yet clear if he was alive or dead.
"Man down!" was the cry heard 'round the course,
While my father played on, showing no remorse.

He played his next shot, and then another three,
When a mob began to form around him and me.
I wanted to leave but my father insisted we stay,
As the ambulance came and took the victim away.

As the crowd grew larger and filled with unrest,
My father shanked another shot off some guy's chest!
This stubborn man raised me and taught me a lot,
But I know that some wars are better not fought.

He's planning to stay because this man has no fear,
But I'm not dying in vain, I'm outta here!

FORE SCORE

The chip you pulled,
The chip you skulled.
The putt that skipped,
The putt that lipped.
Add 'em up and it's four
Extra shots on your score!

GRAY AREAS

The thing about this game
Is you can't believe what people claim.
Some lie about how low they score
And then there's the ten that's really a four.
In both cases they are a liar
One lies low and one lies higher.
But in a wager there is one clear rule
You play the vanity index for a fool.

FINANCIAL DECISIONS

This damn game
My life is not the same.
These green fees
Bring me to my knees.
It really isn't funny
I'm running out of money.
To golf or to eat?
How about you just treat?

THE SINGLE

You're threesome is set, you're ready to go
And then the pro shop adds some rando.
You don't want to judge a book by it's cover
But sometimes you should, as you're about to discover.

He says, "I guess I'm playing with you guys"
As he approaches the tee with a wild look in his eyes.
He has ancient persimmon woods in his bag
And a golf towel that's clearly an old dish rag.

He states, "I come from a family of lumberjacks"
Then announces he'll be teeing off from the blacks.
He steps to the tee and your heart fills with dread
As you watch him top his drive ten yards ahead.

He swears that he was crushing on the driving range
Then blames the bad shot on a recent swing change.
His next shot is somehow even worse than the first
Then he yells at his club and claims that it's cursed.

You still haven't teed off and he's on shot number three
It seems a six hour round is your new destiny.
Your group wonders if anything can save your souls
Because you're stuck with this clown for 17 more holes.

And then it happens, an amazing stroke of luck
The universe helps you get rid of this schmuck...
Off in the distance you hear someone yell "Fore!"
You hear the sound of The Single hitting the floor...
There's a lump on his head that he can't ignore
And you don't have to play with him anymore!

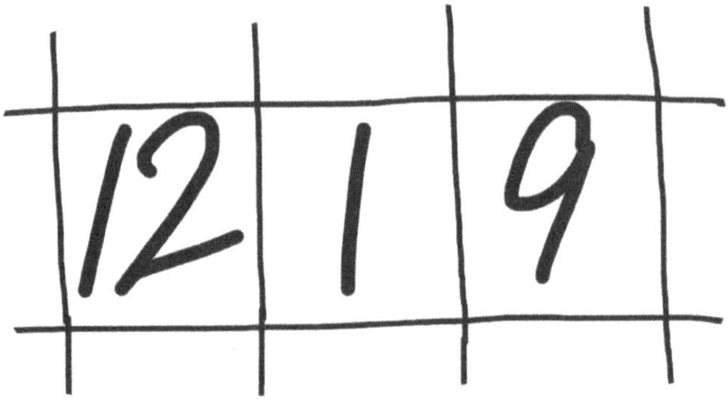

EVEN A BLIND SQUIRREL

I was there when you shot one-twenty-four
It took some time to add up the score
But I signed the card and it's in a case
Why? Because you got an ace!

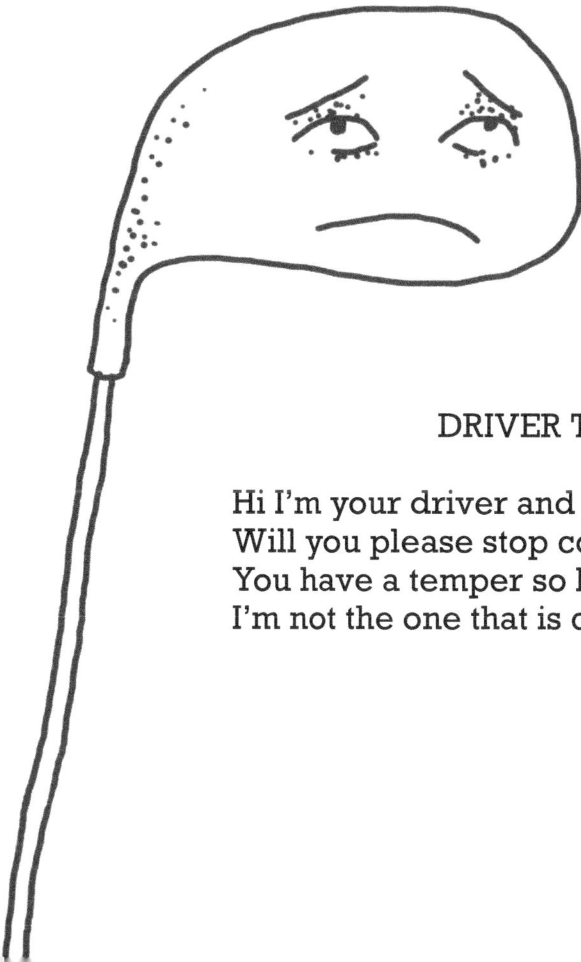

DRIVER THOUGHTS

Hi I'm your driver and I have a plea
Will you please stop constantly cursing at me?
You have a temper so I'll say this nice
I'm not the one that is causing your slice.

EARLY TO RISE

Your alarm clock goes off and you start cursin',
You've never been much of a morning person.
Every bone in your body urges you to hit snooze,
But your mind won't allow it, there's too much to lose.

You're up but the sun isn't, that doesn't seem right,
As you slip out of bed in the dark of the night.
Four thirty a.m. is an ungodly hour,
You think to yourself as you turn on the shower.

But you have somewhere important that you must be,
And you'll be damned if you're late getting to the first tee!

SOMETIMES

Sometimes the putts go in
Sometimes it's for the win!
Sometimes it's to make the cut
But usually you just miss the putt.

DOWNHILL SLIDER

I need you to do what I think you will do,
I don't want any surprises from you.
You're breaking hard left, that much is sure,
But will you be bumpy or will you roll pure?

If I hit you too hard you're way past the hole,
But if my touch is too light I'll lose all control.
I think I can see where you're gonna curl up,
But if I'm a half an inch wrong you'll lip the cup.

O' downhill slider, why must you exist?
Of all the shots in golf you're the worst on my list!
What am I gonna do, you've got in my head,
Ah what the hell, I'll just chip it instead.

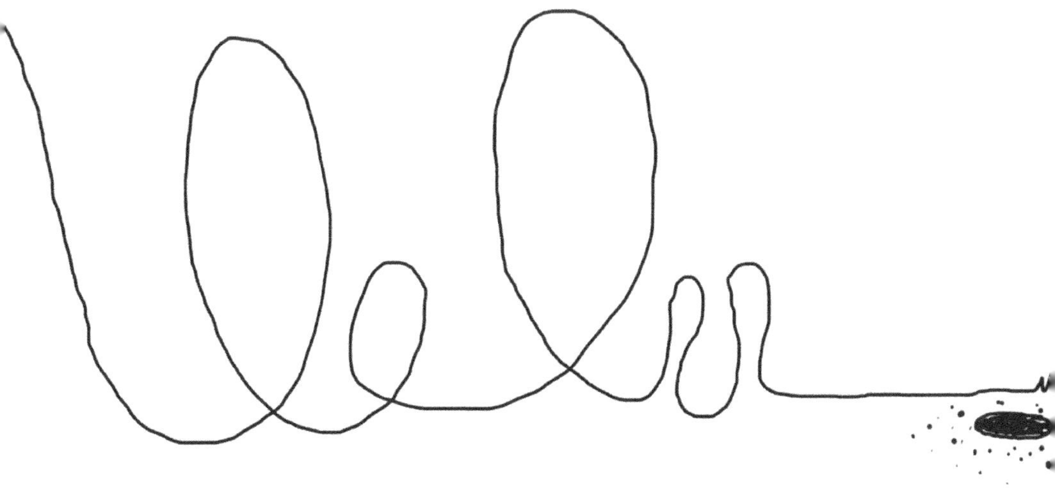

DON'T ASK, DON'T TELL

What is my index? I'd rather not say,
Lately things haven't been going my way.
Besides, I'd rather not be labeled,
Forget handicaps, my game is disabled.

BY THE NUMBERS

A hole in 1
is so much fun
But I'd rather do
a par five in 2
A good hole for me?
around plus 3
But the number I use more
is yelling "Fore!"

CLUB ENVY

I feel the envy coming and try to rise above it,
After all, I was always taught that you shouldn't covet.
But I have been playing with some pretty beat up sticks,
And my buddy just threw down a small fortune at Dick's.

He got the latest driver with the custom carbon face,
The engineers that built it used to work in aerospace.
His three-wood is the same and his hybrid is sublime,
Just those three clubs alone cost more than a dime.

And then there are his irons, a set perfect and pure,
Comparing them to mine makes me feel so insecure.
His wedges are amazing and his putter is the best,
I am filling up with jealousy that cannot be repressed.

But then we play our round and I watch him hit his ball,
And his big investment doesn't seem to pay off at all.
He still hits a nasty slice and his distance is the same,
The only difference now is there aren't clubs he can blame!

And then my envy goes away and I start to feel upbeat,
But now I worry for my buddy - I hope he kept his receipt!

ACHIEVABLE GOALS

You planned to play smart,
Got off to a bad start.
A triple and a quad,
A few choice words for God.
Now your new goal?
Get to the 19th hole!

"CHARITY" GOLF

Handicaps are for parity
But if a tournament is for charity
Don't expect much honesty
The winning score'll be a 53!

A TOUGH LIFE

I'm a broke tee,
Nobody cares about me.
I didn't think things could get much lower
Until I met that lawn mower.

A PRUDENT DECISION

I lost another ProV1
I hate it 'cause they cost a ton.
Maybe I don't have this right
I should switch to Top Flite!

MR. BABA-BOOEY

We hear you on the course from at least a mile away,
But you don't have anything interesting to say.
Between sips of beer you scream and you shout,
You yell "Get in the hole!" on shots 150 out.

You like to run and form a circle around the ball,
And you yell "Mashed potatoes!" for no reason at all.
You scream "You da man!" at players you don't know,
And save "Baba-Booey!" for when you try to steal the show.

We love to hate you, because you are such a clown,
And there's dozens of you all over, in each and every town.
We know this for certain because we hear you every week,
Shouting in the background as the announcers try to speak.

Mr. Baba-Booey has multiplied throughout the years,
He'll never go away, he's like a gopher it appears.
But perhaps there's a way we can solve this crazy puzzle,
Why don't we just invent a Mr. Baba-Booey muzzle?!

SELF AWARENESS

Hole in one? Not for me.
I'm lucky if I'm on in three.
Hole in ten? That sounds right.
Golf's not my game, it's my plight.

SICK DAY

Chunks, hacks and shanks,
It's just another day.
But you still give thanks,
You called in sick to play!

MAYBE IT'S ME?

I really thought
These new clubs I bought
Would help my game.
Here's the thing
It's still my swing
So the results are still the same.

TEETER-TOTTER

Golf is fun when you're making shots
And all you have are positive thoughts.
But when the bogies trade with birds
Out come the four-letter words.

UNSOLICITED ADVICE

Tell me again about turning my hips,
Oh please don't stop giving me tips.
Seriously now, not joking around,
You and I have played our last round.

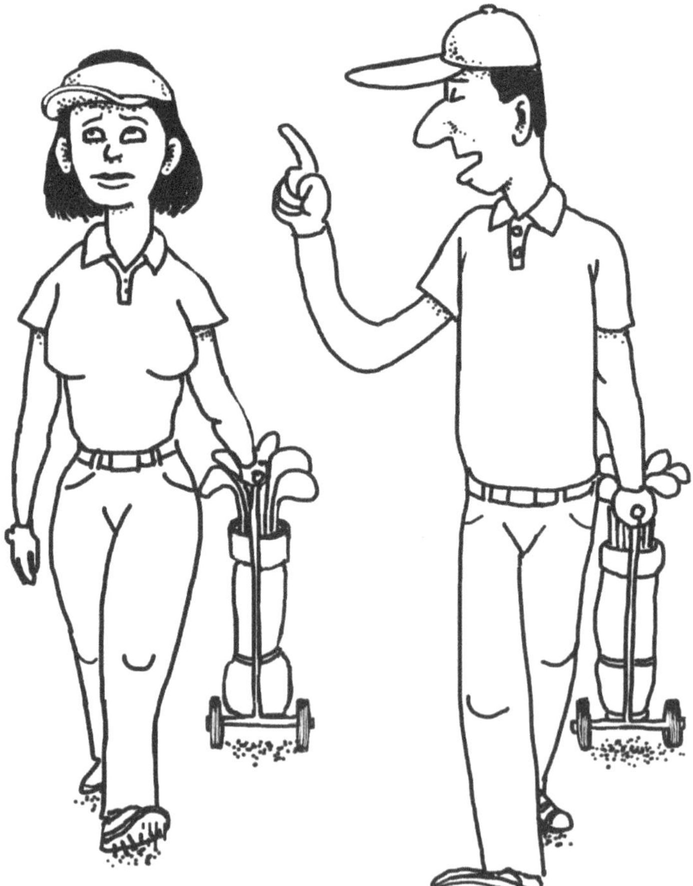

UNIVERSAL TRUTH

In many ways golf is like life
It's also a lot like my wife;
I know what I want when I set the tee
But the golf ball doesn't listen to me!

PLAYING THROUGH IT

Golf on the mind and on the brain,
Golf causing trouble and causing pain.
Hip degenerating, back feeling strain,
But a 7 iron can double as a cane!

THE BEST

A club in one hand,
A beer in the other,
A round of golf with you and your brother.
You realize as you reminisce,
It doesn't get any better than this.

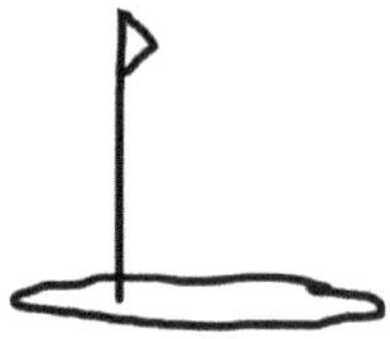

THE THING ABOUT THE SWING

A beautiful swing is a beautiful thing
And leads to a beautiful score.
An ugly slice is like a roll of the dice
And leads to yelling "Fore!"

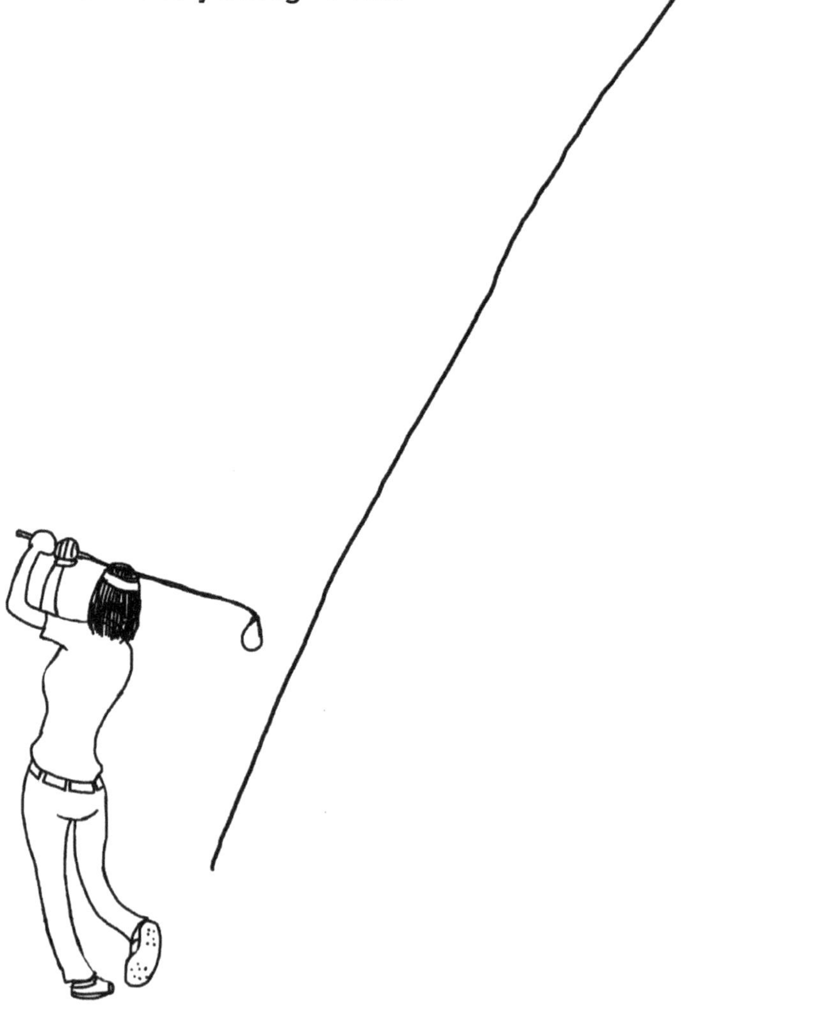

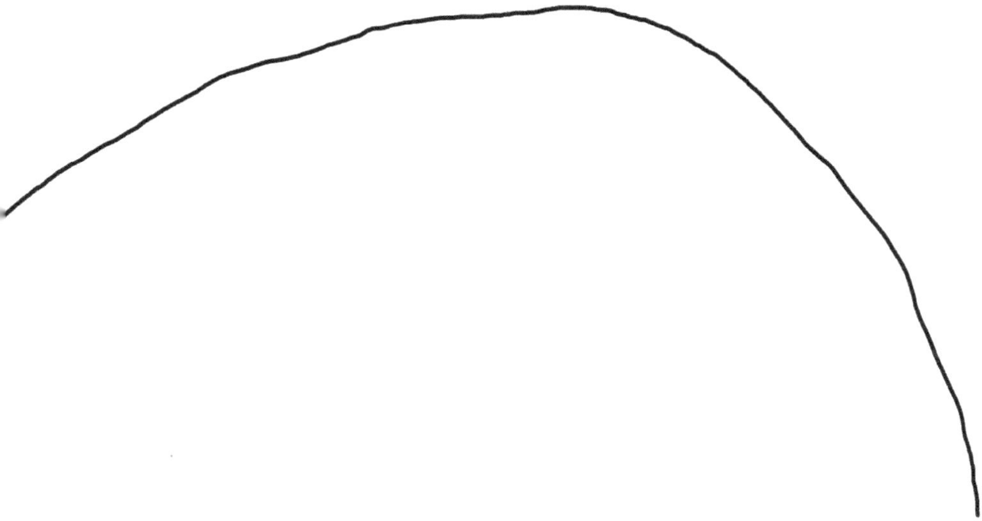

THE MOST USELESS TOOL

Sometimes I feel like a fool
For carrying a divot tool.
The greens have no price to pay
When you can't hit 'em from more than 50 yards away!

THE LIFE OF A DIVOT

I'm a fairway divot and I need a hand,
Could you please cover me with sand?
Soon I'll fill in and grow all the way back,
At least until I'm ruined by the next hack.

THE CHUNK

70 yards in, you're feeling great,
This'll make up for carding that 8.
You take a swing, gentle and true…
And chunk it 10 yards ahead of you.

SAY WHAT?

Hope, soaring through the air,
Fading to despair...
Cutting in a hurry,
Now slicing with fury!
White stakes say O.B.
Your partner says, "Re-tee!"

STAY READY

Your clubs, your shoes and a collared shirt,
Sunscreen and a hat doesn't hurt.
In your car everywhere you go,
Because hey, you never know…

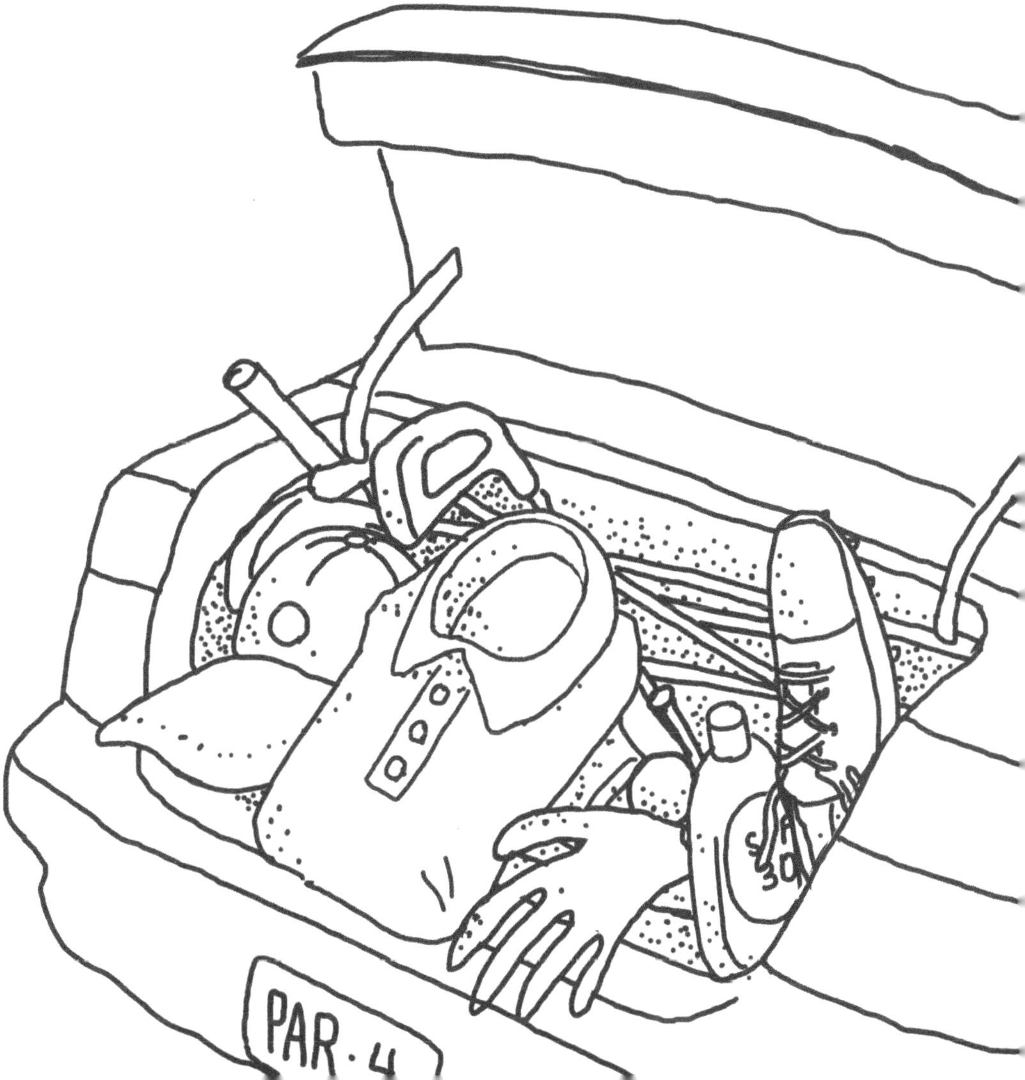

A SAND STORY

Sand, sand, I can't stand,
I prefer much firmer land;
Because my shots never go as planned,
I hate hitting out of sand!

OOPS!

Oh great, you're running late
Gotta be there soon, tee time's at noon!
You're almost there, with time to spare
But what a drag, you forgot your bag!

OUT OF YOUR HANDS

Blues or whites, walk or ride
These are things you must decide.
Straight or slice, fairway or lake
These are choices the Golf Gods make!

PERSPECTIVE

You give, you take,
The good, the bad,
The trap, the lake,
You're sad, you're mad,
But then your fury goes away,
Cause you're supposed to be at work today!

NOTHING TO SEE HERE

Balls sailing through the air,
Balls flying everywhere.
But you don't find this to be strange,
Because you're at the driving range.

MAYBE, JUST MAYBE

You hope, you pray,
Maybe you'll be okay.
Just a few more feet,
Would be so sweet.
But your hopes are gone in a flash,
When you see the splash.

LOSSES

You pray and you hope
But then you must cope.
Yeah, you never say never
But you can't hold on forever…
It's a four-dollar cost, your ball is lost.

GOOD ADVICE

Golf is fun but golf is tough
Especially from the rough.
So if you wanna enjoy the sport
Keep it in the grass that's short.

LOVE HATE

Children love a snowman,
They build them in their yard.
Golfers hate a snowman,
They mark them on their card.

GOLF PHILOSOPHY

The shots you make
Are the shots you take.
The shots you miss
...are also the shots you take.

FROST DELAY

I have a busy day today,
But I really need to get away,
If I slip out early I can play,
But my plan is ruined by a frost delay!

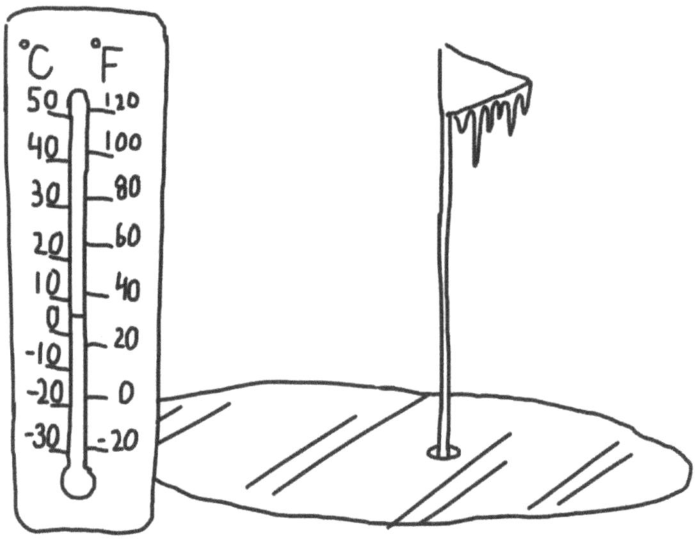

NEVER, USUALLY, ALWAYS

I have NEVER had a hole in one,
I want to 'cause it seems like fun.
I have NEVER finished under par,
But twenty shots over ain't too far.

I USUALLY lose more than one ball,
I buy a box and lose 'em all.
I USUALLY three putt several holes,
One and two putts are lofty goals.

But I ALWAYS have fun on the course,
Though I need to learn to 'use the force.'
And I ALWAYS love to play the game,
Life without it wouldn't be the same.

MEMBERS ONLY

My local muni has been letting me down,
The fairways are all less green than brown.
And you can't get many putts to fall,
If they all bounce more than a basketball.
But there's a private course that's nearby,
And I had an idea that I thought I'd try…

I'd wear my most expensive shirt,
Tuck it in to hide the dirt.
Wear some pants and shine my shoes,
And see if I could pull off a ruse.
I figured I could not go wrong,
If I just acted like I belong.
And so I walked up to the gate,
Said my tee time was at eight.
The guard was clearly not impressed,
He asked, "Of which member are you a guest?"
I thought I might have a chance still,
When I blurted out, "Mr. Underhill."
He just smirked and said, "Nice try,
It's members only and I must comply."
And so I turned around to leave,
But I still had one trick up my sleeve.
I returned later around sunset,
I wasn't ready to give up yet.
Because I don't quit on my goals…
So I hopped a fence and played three holes!

DEATH MATCH

Me and my buddy played a match,
I'm a ten and he's a scratch.
We had a wager I thought was fair,
But soon I was in deep despair.
He called a hammer and a press,
And put me under lots of stress.
I made bogeys while he scored,
And lost more than I could afford.
He bought me a drink at the bar,
But then he drove off in my car!

EMOTIONS

That's it!
I quit!
This game's no fun
Me oh my!
Did I?
A hole in one?
Forget everything I said before,
I'm not quitting anymore.

FOUR LETTER WORDS

Chip and putt are four-letter words,
But on the course others are heard.
When a chip or putt goes awry,
They look up to the sky,
And let 'em fly!

FAIRWAY BUNKER

Oh fairway bunker I loathe you,
I need to get on in two;
I pray somehow I'll pick it clean,
And be dancing on the green!

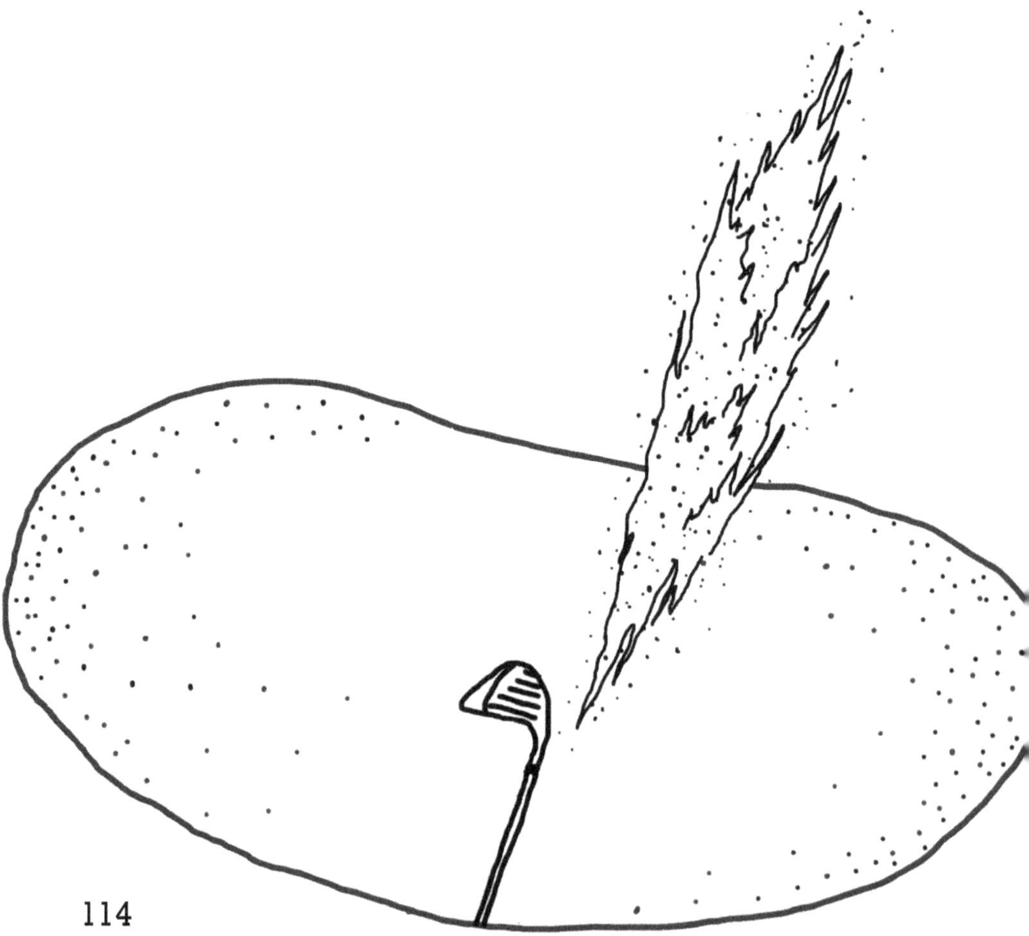

COMING UP SHORT

Roll… roll… get in the hole!
No! Don't start slowing, you gotta keep going!
The line was straight and true
I just needed one more inch from you…

COJONES

You bought one sleeve, should be enough
Then you lost two in the rough.
Now there's a lake you must fly
But you don't have the balls to try!

MUNI BALL WASHER

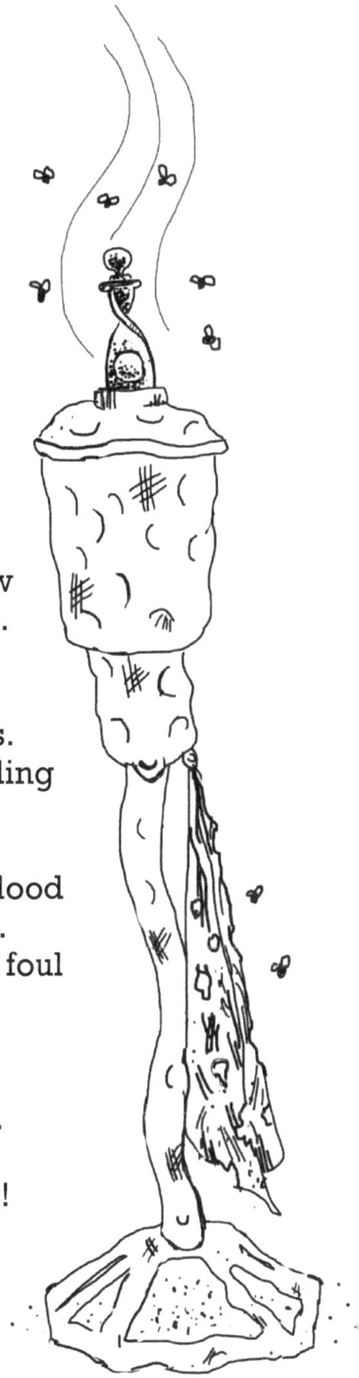

There was a time when you were new
When golfers weren't disgusted by you.
But that time has passed and we all know
That your expiration date was years ago.

You have a stench that really reeks
Your water's been stale for seven weeks.
The only thing at which you are succeeding
Is as a center for mosquito breeding.

Your handle's cracked and has drawn blood
And your bristles are all filled with crud.
And there are few things in the world as foul
As that dangling rag you call a towel.

So thank you but I think I'll pass
I prefer my ball to be stained with grass.
And if I change my mind in a bit
It would be cleaner to just use some spit!

SCRAMBLED

I'm not sore in defeat,
But I hate the scramble cheat.
Sixteen under? Good for you,
At least my score's actually true!

CONFUCIUS SAYS

The young man hits far.
The old man hits straight.
The old man shoots par.
The young man an eight.

THE BALL THIEF

Hey man, did you pick up my ball?
It hit a tree and I saw it fall
I know it should be right here
Can you just make it reappear?
Look buddy, I know you did it
Will you be a man and just admit it?
No? Okay here's what we'll do
I will take something from you
But it's something you can't see
'Cause I just took your dignity!

MAYBE TOMORROW

Ball in the breeze,
Ball in the reeds.
Ball in the trees,
Ball in the weeds.
Ball in the fairway? Not today!

WORLD'S SLOWEST GOLFER

A practice swing, then another
Then he walks behind his ball.
If he wasn't my wife's brother
I wouldn't be out here at all.

He finally comes to address
And inhales deeply four times.
I've seen faster games of chess
And heard shorter podcasts on crimes...

He chunks it forward twenty yards
Then starts the whole routine again.
We're going to need security guards
Cause behind us are four angry men!

When we finally make it to the green
Things go from bad to worse.
I've never heard anything as obscene
As what I heard the men behind us curse.

We wave the angry men on through
But our snail's pace doesn't change.
And then it's just like deja vu
We have another nasty exchange.

I tell him he should play faster
But he doesn't seem to care.
Playing with him is such a disaster
Because he isn't self-aware.

Groups played through on each par three
And even one on a par five.
I've moved faster at the DMV
Waited less for mail to arrive!

Then at last there was a saving of our souls
Mercifully our round was done.
We didn't finish after eighteen holes
It was the setting of the sun!

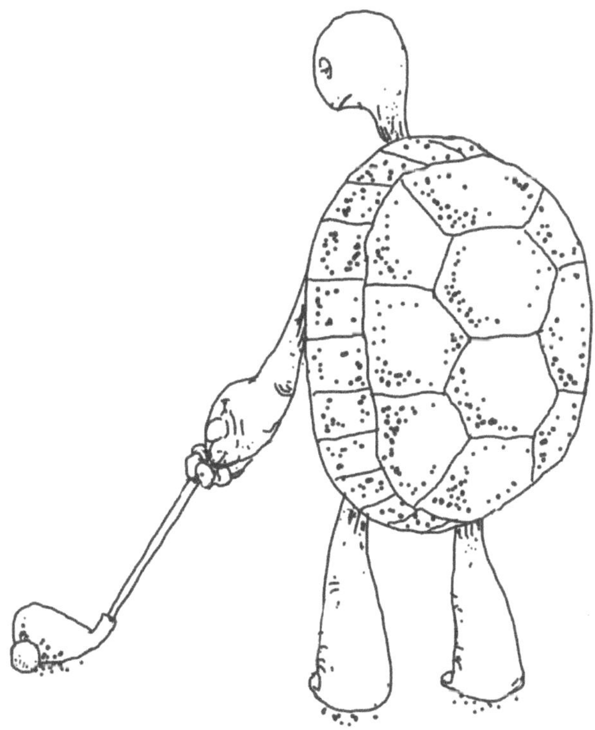

THE GOLF GODS

From high above
They watch and they judge,
They are mostly fair
But they do hold a grudge.
If you sand your divots
And don't walk through a line,
Don't tee off in front of birdies
And you should be just fine.
But if you break the rules
And if you make them mad,
They will make you pay
And the punishment is bad.
Balls get stuck in trees
And putts start to lip out,
The Golf Gods want penance
And you must be devout.
You sacrifice a golf ball
When you hit it in the lake,
But the Golf Gods want more
They want to see you break.
You ask them what you did
You ask them for mercy,
But they are not listening
And a bad bounce goes O.B.
The round is almost over
And you still try to repent,
The Golf Gods are still angry
Will they ever be content?
Then you finally you get a break
The clouds start clearing up,
You bounce one off a sprinkler
To three feet from the cup!

WORM BURNER

I try to hit the ball high in the air
But instead I give the worms a scare.
I've never had a shot stuck in a tree
How someone does that's a mystery to me.
My ball flight never gets above my knees
My best launch angle is eleven degrees.
But there's more to golf than to elevate
My secret weapon? I can hit it straight!

THE YIPS

You were playing fine
On the front nine
Every shot was pure…
Your game was strong
Now something's wrong
And you can't find a cure.

There is a word
For what's occurred
And you let it cross your lips…
You're face-to-face
With a sudden case
Of the dreaded yips.

Your only thought
Before each shot
Is to make them go away…
You try your best
But you fail the test
The yips are here to stay!

DELUSIONAL

I grab my balls and I hit the course
I swing my driver with massive force
John Daly ain't got nothin' on me
Two-thirty off the tee!

INDEX

To those that listened to the early poems and said, “That should be in a book.”
Thank you for the support.
To those that said, “That’s a terrible idea. It will never work.”
Thank you for the motivation.
To my family, friends and golf buddies - thank you.
Special thanks to Scott Bailey for managing to get me to finish.
And to Morgan Wellborn for his fine work, many thanks.

Barney Goldstein

www.ingramcontent.com/pod-product-compliance
Ingram Content Group UK Ltd.
Pitfield, Milton Keynes, MK11 3LW, UK
UKHW060126010826
14089UKWH00022B/267/J

9 798988 701903